INTRODUCTION

This book is intended as an aid to those who teach 10 to 14 age group, though we think it may also be helpful to the teacher who has a class of older but less able pupils.

In preparing the book we have drawn upon our own experience as, we hope, typical Home Economics teachers and have tried to make it the sort of teaching aid we ourselves would like to have available to us. It is not a text book in the conventional sense, nor is it a prepared step-by-step course, rather it is a series of prepared activity sheets that can be selected by the teacher to stimulate the interest of the class and encourage the involvement of the pupils. There are suggestions for homework, easily prepared lessons for supply or probationary teachers, lively ways of introducing new topics, and ideas for work for an absent colleague's class. The suggestions we have made can readily be used as part of a teacher's own course of lessons and, of course, the concept is designed to enable the teacher to copy and distribute the individual activity sheets.

We hope that our efforts will help to make Home Economics a more appealing subject for the pupils and to lighten the burden of preparation and innovation on the teacher.

JANE HEPBURN
AND
ELIZABETH PRETSWELL

© Collins Educational

First published in 1990

Reprinted 1992

Any educational institution that has purchased one copy of this publication may make duplicate copies for use exclusively within that institution. Permission does not extend to reproduction, storage in a retrieval system or transmittal, in any form or by any means, electronic, mechanical, photocopying, recording or otherwise, of duplicate copies for loaning, renting or selling to any other institution without the prior consent in writing of the publisher.

Published by Collins Educational, an imprint of HarperCollins*Publishers*, 77-85 Fulham Palace Road, Hammersmith, London W6 8JB.

Printed by Holmes McDougall Ltd., Edinburgh

ISBN 0 00 329470 6

RESOURCES REQUIRED FOR EACH ACTIVITY

Activity	Reference Books	Coloured Pens/Pencils	Glue/Scissors	Magazines	Paper	Recipe Books (R)	Samples of Fabric (O)	Mail Order Catalogues	Hand Sewing Equipment	Travel Brochures	Mirror	Group work possible
HYGIENE												
1. Snappy Slogans												
2. Clean Scene	□	🏠			📄							
3. Problem Page	□				📄							
4. The Ups and Downs of Hygiene	□	🏠										🧍
5a/b Cobweb Cafe					📄							
SAFETY												
1. A School for Safety		🏠			📄							
2. Better Safe than Sorry	□	🏠			📄							🧍
3. The Search for Safety	□				📄							
4. Be on your Guard.		🏠			📄			▤				
FOOD AND DIET												
1. Mini Meals		🏠			📄							
2. Think Thin	□	🏠			📄							
3 Make a meal of it.		🏠			📄	R						
4. Waste not Want not.					📄	R						
5. Creative Cocktails		🏠			📄							
6. Food Fads	□				📄	R						🧍
7a/b The Good Store Guide		🏠										
8a/b Let's get Quizzical											💧	
9. Packing for a Picnic					📄	R						🧍
10a/b Teenage Diet Dominoes	□	🏠			📄							🧍
HEALTH AND FITNESS												
1. Problems for the Plumps		🏠			📄							
2. Fitness is fun					📄							
3. Body Talk	□		✂	🛍	📄							
4. Be a sport	□	🏠	✂	🛍	📄	R	O	▤				
HOME CARE												
1a/b Spick'n'Span												
2. Sweet Dreams		🏠			📄			▤				
3. Rubbish Recycled		🏠			📄							🧍
CONSUMER												
1. Designer Dilemma		🏠			📄							
2. Commercial Capers	□	🏠			📄							🧍
3. Costa del Packet	□									☀		
4. Teenage Temptations		🏠			📄			▤				🧍
5. Noel, Noel					📄			▤				
6a/b All the Fun of the Fair		🏠			📄							🧍
FABRIC AND CLOTHES CARE												
1. On the Touch Line	□		✂				O					
2. Fault Flattery		🏠	✂		📄			▤				
3. A Stitch in Time							O		🪡			
4. Dress to Impress		🏠			📄							
5a/b Walking Wardrobe		🏠	✂		📄		O	▤				🧍
FAMILY LIFE												
1. Community Spirit	□	🏠			📄							
2. One of the Gang					📄							
3. Black Magic		🏠	✂		📄	R						🧍
4. Toying with Trouble	□	🏠		🛍	📄			▤				
5. Tell Tale		🏠	✂	🛍	📄							
6. I love to go a Wandering	□	🏠			📄	R						
7. Its Party Time		🏠	✂	🛍	📄	R						🧍

KEY

- □ Reference Books
- 🏠 Coloured Pens/Pencils
- ✂ Glue/Scissors
- 🛍 Magazines
- 📄 Paper
- R Recipe Books
- O Samples of Fabric
- ▤ Mail Order Catalogues
- 🪡 Hand Sewing Equipment
- ☀ Travel Brochures
- 💧 Mirror
- 🧍 Group work possible

SNAPPY SLOGANS

"Body Maintenance", a firm which sells body care products, is running a competition to find the snappiest slogans to advertise its main products.

Write a slogan for each of the cartoons below.

HYGIENE 1

CLEAN SCENE

Design a sticker to illustrate each of the kitchen hygiene rules given below.

NO SMOKING IN THE KITCHEN

NO PETS ALLOWED IN THE KITCHEN

Now think of another kitchen hygiene rule and design an appropriate sticker.

HYGIENE 2

Problem Page?

There are too many volunteers to help with the school magazine. The post of agony aunt/uncle will be filled by the person who answers the following problems in the most helpful and detailed way. You are desperate to get this post.

Dear _ _ _ _ _ _ _
My shoulders get covered in little white flakes. Some people at school laugh at me and ask if it has been snowing. Can you tell me what this is and how I can get rid of it?
                    Yours desperately,
                    Dan Druff.

Dear Dan Druff,

Dear _ _ _ _ _ _
In a few weeks I have an interview for a weekend job in a café. In the advert for the job it states that a high standard of personal hygiene will be required. How can I prepare myself for this interview?
                    Yours hopefully
                    E. Gertoserve.

Dear E. Gertoserve,

Dear _ _ _ _ _ _
I am a member of a badminton club. A boy I really like goes to the club. Each week after the game I dash up to the café without bothering to have a shower, so that I don't miss him. Although he's friendly when we're playing he always avoids me in the café. What am I doing wrong?
                    Yours sadly,
                    Bo D. Odour

Dear Miss Odour,

HYGIENE 3

The Ups and Downs of Hygiene

Make up a game on the grid provided by writing a good hygienic practice at the bottom of each toothbrush and an unhygienic practice at the top of each dirty comb, e.g. no 47 has been done for you. The game is based on the rules of SNAKES AND LADDERS but it needs a more appropriate name. Fill in the name at the top of the game. If you have time try out your game with a few friends.

43	44	45	46	Did not 47 shower after P.E.	48	49
42	41	40	39	38	37	36
29	30	31	32	33	34	35
28	27	26	25	24	23	22
15	16	17	18	19	20	21
14	13	12	11	10	9	8
1	2	3	4	5	6	7

HYGIENE 4

Cobweb Café is an ideal breeding ground for germs.
Any food cooked and served in these unhygienic surroundings could cause food poisoning and lead to the closure of the café.
Cobweb Café is owned and run by your friend who is going on holiday. You have been asked to run the café for a fortnight and decide to have a major clean up campaign.
Identify the unhygienic areas in Cobweb Café.
Draw a germ at work at each of these areas.

HYGIENE 5a

Cobweb Cafe

TIME FOR ACTION
Listed here are the jobs which you must do to turn Cobweb Café into The Delightful Diner.

Put the jobs in logical order

Bake scones

Make tea and coffee

Polish floor

Unlock door and put out the "open" sign

Empty and clean waste bins

Clean sink and pour bleach down drain

Wash down work surfaces and tables with disinfectant

Throw out chipped and cracked crockery

Wash floor

Wash dirty dishes

Make sandwiches

Sweep floor

Set tables

Remove pets

Clean windows

Teenagers often complain that they have nothing to do and nowhere to go. A café that opened in the evenings and at weekends would be an ideal meeting place for them, yet there are very few cafés which encourage teenagers.

You have been chosen to represent the local teenagers at a meeting with the owner of The Delightful Diner. Write down all the points which you will put forward in an effort to persuade him to open his café to teenagers.

He has already indicated that he has reservations based on these points:

• teenagers are noisy and disruptive • they want loud music all the time

• their parents will complain when they are late home

• they will want to sit for a long time without spending much money

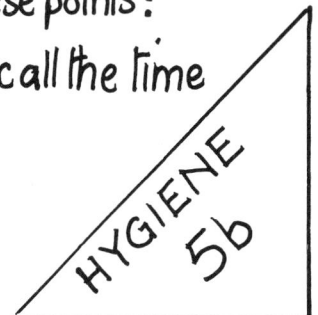

HYGIENE 5b

a and 5b

A SCHOOL FOR SAFETY

Invent two characters who are to star in the monthly newsletter produced by the school safety officer. One of your characters has to be "accident prone" and the other "safety conscious."

1. Draw and name your two characters.
2. Choose one of the titles below and make up a cartoon strip using your two characters.

Fool in the Pool   **Playground Pranks**   **Kitchen Capers**

SAFETY 1

Better safe than sorry

Far too many accidents happen in and around the home. These are often due to carelessness, negligence, tiredness, impatience and lack of knowledge. Many of the accidents could be prevented or their results made less serious if everyone had a sound knowledge of <u>HOME SAFETY</u> and <u>BASIC FIRST AID.</u>

DON'T DELAY LEARN TODAY!

Complete this alphabetical list of accidents that might occur in and around the home. The first three have been done for you.

    a: asphyxiation with plastic bag.

    b: burn with hot iron.

    c: cut by broken bottle in garden.

The main types of houshold accidents are 1) FALLS, 2) POISONING, 3) BURNS AND SCALDS AND 4) CUTS.

CHOOSE ONE OF THE ABOVE TYPES OF ACCIDENTS.

① Write a set of rules on how to prevent this type of accident in and around the home.

② Make a list of the age groups most likely to be involved in this type of accident.

③ Design a poster showing one of the causes of this type of accident.

④ Make up a short sketch (play) that demonstrates one cause of this type of accident and the first aid treatment to be given. If there is time, act out your sketch with your classmates.

SAFETY 2

The Search for Safety

Find the answers to the following clues in the wordsearch below. The answers may be found in straight lines running horizontally, vertically, diagonally, forwards or backwards. As you find each one, circle it in pen or pencil.

1. A child who plays with a plastic bag may _____

2. This type of appliance should not be taken into the bathroom.

3. Use to keep children away from fires.

4. Essential in every home.

5. One service you can get if you dial 999.

6. Children should not leave these on the stairs.

7. A peanut can cause a toddler to _____

8. A wet burn.

9. Never put a plug in a socket with these.

10. Keep this in a high, locked cupboard.

11. Use, wash and store this piece of equipment with great care.

12. Probably the most dangerous room in the house.

E	S	U	F	F	O	C	A	T	E	B	W
M	L	S	I	I	F	H	O	T	O	O	E
E	A	E	R	R	T	O	I	S	P	Y	T
R	M	F	C	S	E	K	M	C	O	S	S
G	P	I	N	T	N	E	E	A	I	D	H
E	S	R	E	A	R	A	D	L	L	O	A
N	D	E	H	I	O	I	I	A	S	N	R
S	N	G	C	D	O	L	C	S	I	O	P
I	A	U	T	K	M	S	I	A	C	T	K
E	H	A	I	I	E	M	N	S	L	O	N
T	T	R	K	T	T	P	E	E	R	I	I
O	E	D	A	G	I	R	B	E	R	I	F
P	W	S	T	R	I	F	G	R	E	M	E

USING THE RESOURCE BOOKS AVAILABLE, MAKE UP YOUR OWN CLUES AND WORDSEARCH. CHECK YOUR CLUES AND ANSWERS WITH YOUR TEACHER, THEN TRY IT OUT ON YOUR CLASSMATES.

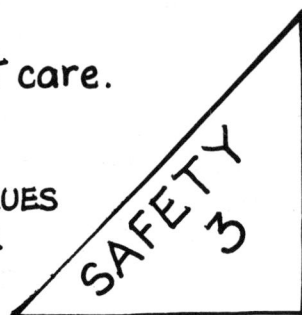

SAFETY 3

BE ON YOUR GUARD

Taking care of your possessions is important at all times but especially when you go on holiday.

USING THE PICTURE CLUES PROVIDED COMPLETE THE CROSSWORD.

ACROSS
1. Your house and possessions should be covered by fire and theft _____. (9)
5. Turn all these off to prevent fire. (7)
6. Turn this off at the main or it could cause a flood. (5)
9. Lock these securely and get someone to double check. (5,3,7)
10. Unwelcome visitors. (8)
12. Lock these away in a safety deposit box on holiday. (9)

DOWN
2. This must be left on if you have food in your fridge/freezer, otherwise turn it off at the main switch. (11)
3. They could be your lookouts if you tell them you are going away. (11)
4. If left lying around, these may help unwelcome visitors to get into the house (7)
7. A leak of this substance could be explosive so turn it off at the mains. (3)
8. If asked, they will call at regular intervals to check that nothing has been disturbed. (6)
11. Pull these out of the sockets before you leave. (5)
13. Switch this safety precaution on, if you have one. (5)

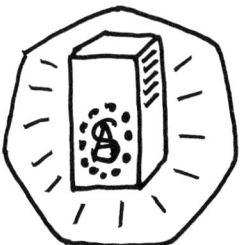

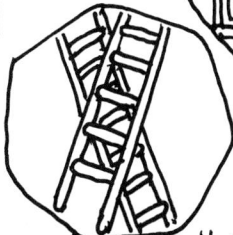

Now make a poster of safety precautions you should follow when going on holiday.
When going on holiday it is wise to take out extra insurance cover for loss or damage to your possessions.
Make a list of all the items you would take on holiday and work out how much it would cost to replace all these things.

SAFETY

Mini Meals

Young children often have to be encouraged to eat their meals. They would far rather play than sit down quietly and eat.

Special foods are produced that are designed to appeal to young children.
For example, potato fries in the shape of letters and spaghetti in the shape of spaceships.

1. Invent some new foods for children.

2. Choose one of the foods that you have invented and design an advert for a magazine to try to sell your new food.

3. Colourful appealing dishes can also encourage children to eat. Design a plate, dish and cup that you think would appeal to young children.

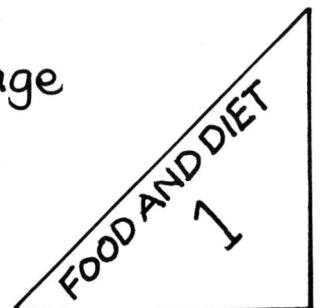

FOOD AND DIET 1

THINK THIN

If the members of the Plump family are to lose weight they will have to alter their diets. If eaten in excess, foods which contain either fat or carbohydrate will cause a body to become overweight. The Plumps will have to cut down on these foods.

• List foods containing fat which begin with the letters in the word "fat",
for example: **F** : French toast,_ _ _ _ _ _
A : avocado, _ _ _ _ _ _ _
T :_ _ _ _ _ _ _ _ _ _

• List foods containing carbohydrate which begin with the letters in the word "carbohydrate", for example;
C : chocolate, cake,_ _ _ _ _ _
A :_ _ _ _ _ _ _ _ _ _ _
R :_ _ _ _ _ _ _ _ _ _ _
B :_ _ _ _ _ _ _ _ _ _ _
:

Help the Plump family to eat sensibly by choosing suitable foods for their meals.

• Mr. Plump is having lunch in the office canteen. What should he choose? Why should he choose these?

MENU

Soup and roll	Sausage rolls
Filled rolls	Pasty and beans
Ham salad	Sausage and chips

Jam sponge and custard
Yogurt   Selection of cakes
Fresh fruit   Tea, coffee

• Mrs Plump tends to eat snacks each day rather than regular meals. She need not cook a fancy meal for herself but she should eat a proper lunch. Suggest three easy lunches which she could prepare.

• Patrick and Penelope take packed lunches to school. Draw and label the contents of their lunch boxes.

PATRICK

PENELOPE

FOOD AND DIET
2

MAKE A MEAL OF IT

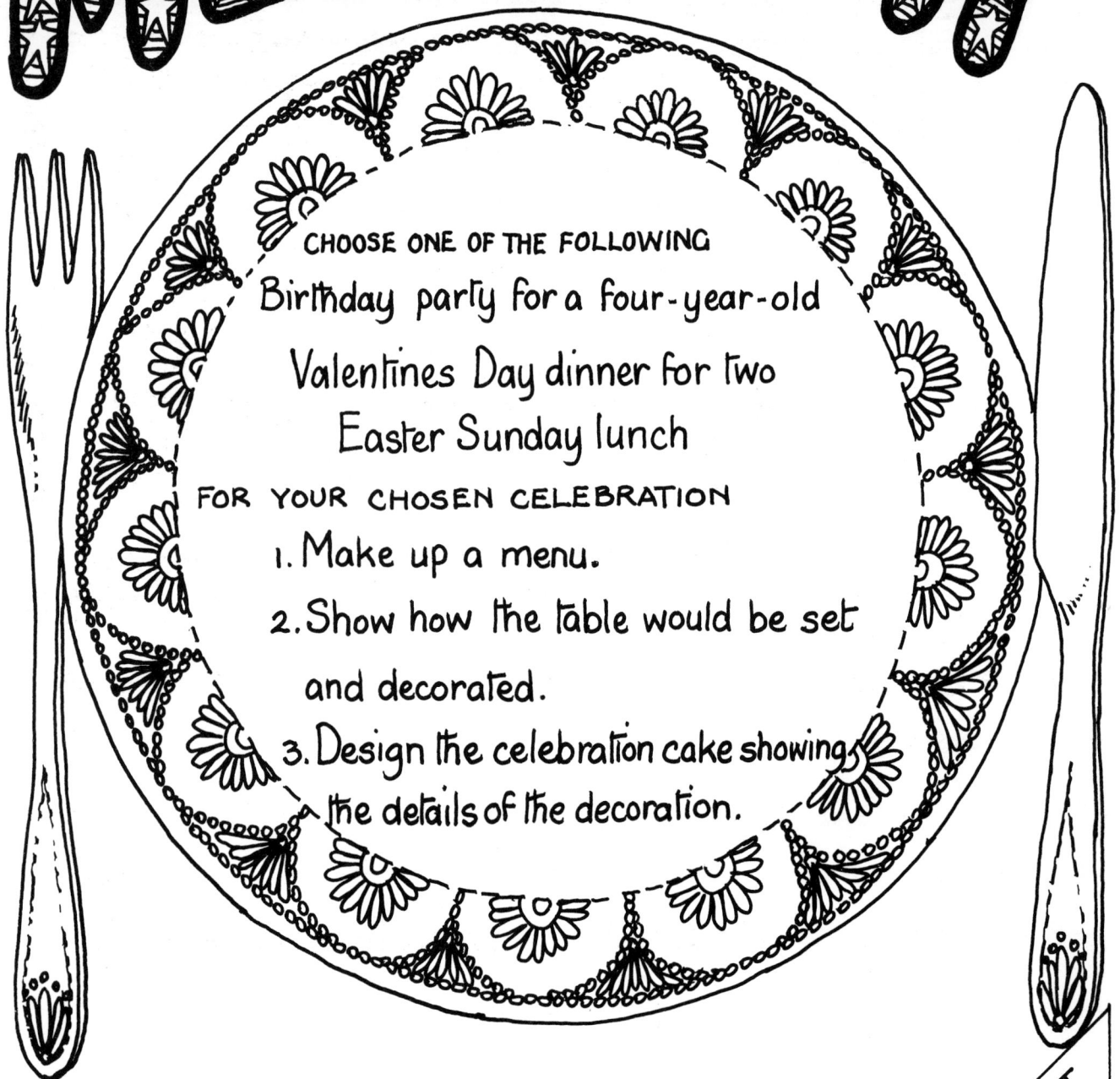

CHOOSE ONE OF THE FOLLOWING

Birthday party for a four-year-old

Valentines Day dinner for two

Easter Sunday lunch

FOR YOUR CHOSEN CELEBRATION

1. Make up a menu.

2. Show how the table would be set and decorated.

3. Design the celebration cake showing the details of the decoration.

FOOD AND DIET 3

Waste not Want not

The school holidays are fast approaching. It is only a week until the end of term and the Home Economics Department need to use up the following ingredients.

MILK Potatoes Apples Rhubarb MINCE

Certain dry ingredients are also available from the main store cupboard

PLAIN FLOUR · PLAIN FLOUR · DRIED FRUIT · SELF RAISING FLOUR · FLOUR · MACARONI

CASTER SUGAR · LONG GRAIN RICE · CURRY POWDER · CHILLI POWDER · SPAGHETTI

PEACHES · TOMATOES · KIDNEY BEANS · GELATINE

Your teacher has asked you to suggest dishes which could be made in the remaining three lessons.

Some of the skills learned throughout the year have to be revised in these three lessons. These skills include chopping, slicing, beating, grating, kneading, rolling, rubbing in, baking, boiling, stewing, whisking, creaming, frying and shaping.

Using recipe books and your own ideas, suggest a dish that could be made in each lesson. For each dish list the ingredients required and the skills revised.

FOOD AND DIET X

CREATIVE COCKTAILS

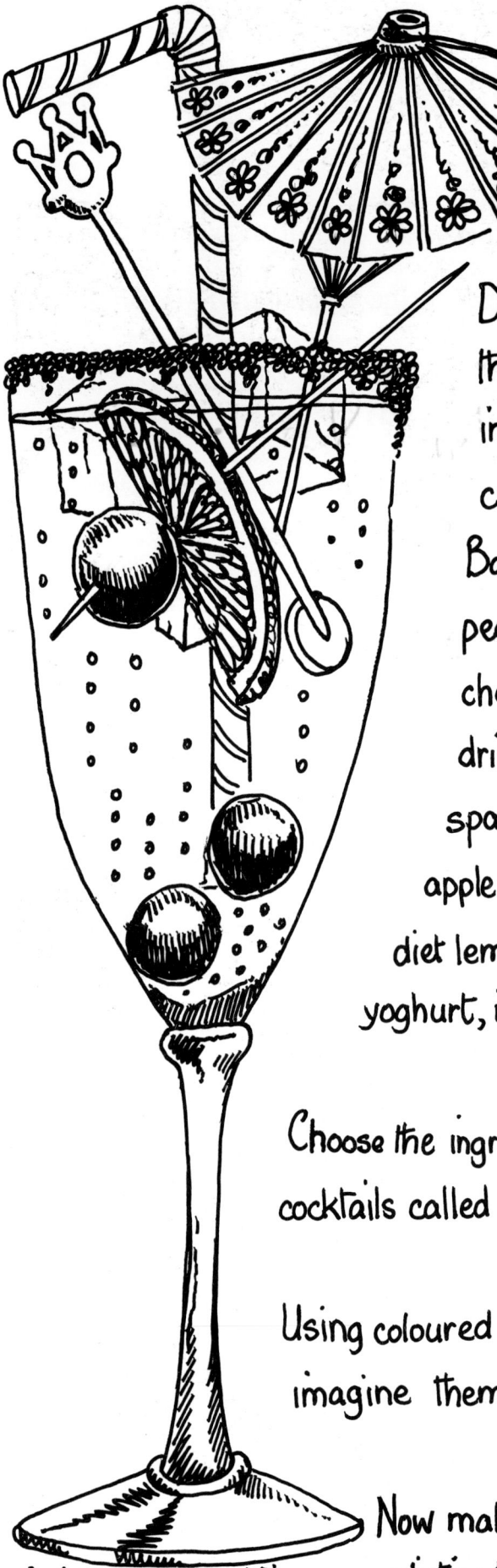

Drinks can be nutritious as well as thirst quenching and tasty. The following ingredients could be used to make creative cocktails.

Bananas, skimmed milk, strawberries, peaches, raspberries, crushed pineapple, cherries, oranges, lemons, puréed carrots, dried fruit, coconut, grated chocolate, sparkling mineral water, fresh orange juice, apple juice, lime juice, red or white grape juice, diet lemonade, soda water, peppermint flavouring, yoghurt, ice cream, various food colourings.

Choose the ingredients you think would be used to make cocktails called
1. Grasshopper
2. Island in the sun.

Using coloured pencils, draw the cocktails as you imagine them being served.

Now make up three cocktails of your own, giving them exciting names, listing their ingredients and drawing how they would be served. Perhaps you could make the most creative cocktails in class, or try them out at home.

FOOD FADS

Assignment 1

Daisy is a diabetic and must be careful about the amount of sugar she eats. Plan a two course meal for Daisy consisting of a main course and a sweet.

Remember that substitute sweeteners can be used instead of sugar.

Assignment 2

Constipated Connie has been told to include a lot of fibre in her diet.

Suggest some suitable biscuits and cakes for Connie to bake.

Assignment 3

Vegetarian Victor is planning a party. He intends to serve a buffet supper. Suggest some vegetarian dishes which he could include in the supper.

Assignment 4

Fred has just had four fillings at the dentist.

It was very painful and Fred never wants another filling.

Plan four packed lunches for filling-fearing Fred.

Assignment 5

Fourteen-year-old Spotty Dotty is worried about her appearance. She feels that she is slightly plump and has too many spots. Cutting down on sugar and fat may help. Two of Spotty Dotty's friends are coming for tea. What should she serve?

FOOD AND DIET

6

THE GOOD STORE GUIDE

Food must be stored correctly to prevent it from going bad or becoming infected. Covering foods protects them from dust and flies. As germs multiply at room temperature food is safer when cool.

FOOD STORAGE GUIDE

FOODS	STORAGE
Dry groceries and tinned foods	Cool dry cupboard
Fruit	Dry airy place e.g. fruit bowl
Salad vegetables	Drawer in refrigerator
Root vegetables	Dry airy place e.g. vegetable rack
Green vegetables	<u>Dark</u>, dry, airy place e.g. wrapped in newspaper in vegetable rack.
Bread	Cool airy place e.g. bread bin
Perishables (foods which go off quickly)	Refrigerator for short periods of time e.g. Milk, yoghurt → 2-3 days Cheese, marg., butter, eggs → 7-10 days Meat, fish → 2 days
Frozen Foods	Freezer or ice box in refrigerator (for short period of time.)

FOOD AND DIET 7a

Here is a holiday menu for 3 days.

	BREAKFAST	LUNCH	TEA
DAY 1	Cornflakes, Toast, margarine, jam Coffee	Ham Salad Yoghurt	Grilled fish, chips and frozen peas Rice pudding
DAY 2	Grapefruit Bacon and egg Coffee	Baked potato with cheese and coleslaw Fresh fruit salad	Chicken and mushroom pie with sweetcorn Stewed apple with Tinned custard
DAY 3	Cornflakes Toast, margarine, jam Coffee	Macaroni and cheese with tomatoes Mint ice cream	Mince, carrots and potatoes Frozen cheesecake

★1. Complete this shopping list for the holiday food. – look at the menu and make a list.

Cornflakes   _ _ _ _ _ _ _ _ _ _ _

Milk   _ _ _ _ _ _ _ _ _ _ _

Bread   _ _ _ _ _ _ _ _ _ _ _

★2. Draw the foods into the correct storage areas in the caravan.

FOOD AND DIET
7b

Let's get Quizzical

1. Find the route to the centre of the maze - the protein spot. Now retrace your path and list all the foods you pass. These foods are rich sources of protein. Protein foods help the body to grow and repair it when necessary.

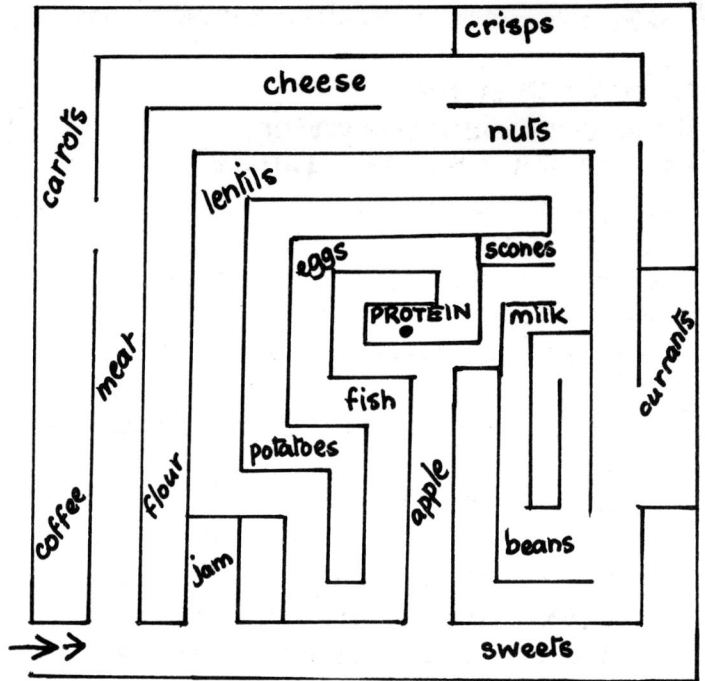

2. Use the following code to name the equipment found in the kitchen.

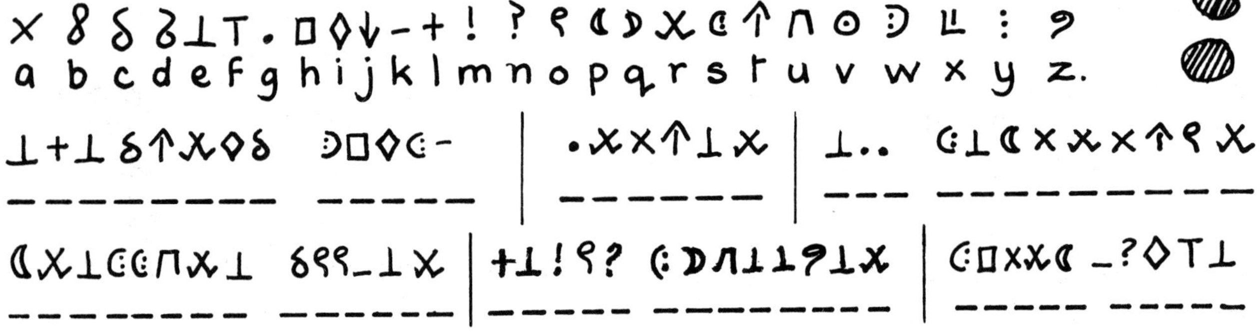

⤬	8	8	3	ⳑ	T	.	▢	◊	⩔	–	+	!	ꝑ	ꝯ	⸦	⸧	⤬	⸦	↑	∩	○	ꓭ	⊔	:	ꝯ
a	b	c	d	e	f	g	h	i	j	k	l	m	n	o	p	q	r	s	t	u	v	w	x	y	z.

⊔+⊔8↑⤬○8 ꓭ▢○�◊– _ _ _ _ _ _ _ _   _ _ _ _ _

.⤬⤬↑⊥⤬ ⊥.. ⸦⊔⸦⤬⤬⤬↑ꝑ⤬ _ _ _ _ _ _   _ _ _   _ _ _ _ _ _ _ _ _

⸦⤬⊥⸦⸦∩⤬⊥ 8ꝑꝯ_⊥⤬ _ _ _ _ _ _ _ _   _ _ _ _ _

+⊥!ꝑꝑ ⸦ꓭ∩⊥⊥ꝑ◊⊥⤬ _ _ _ _ _   _ _ _ _ _ _ _ _

⸦▢⤬⤬⸦ _ꝑ◊⊥⊥ _ _ _ _ _   _ _ _ _ _

Match each piece of equipment with one of the sentences below.

a) Uses steam to cook food very quickly _____

b) Introduces air to foods _____

c) Used for cutting vegetables _____

d) Removes the yolk from the white _____

e) Breaks food up into small pieces _____

f) Removes the juice from the fruit _____

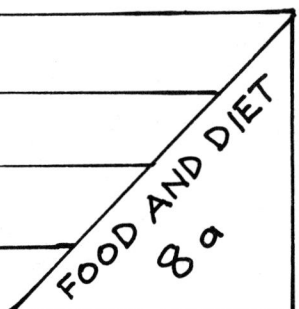

FOOD AND DIET

8 a

Let's get Quizzical

Identify these fruits and vegetables

3 a) _____
b) OK _____
c) rice _____
d) _____
e) _____
f) _____

4 **Use a mirror to find the answers to these questions.**

a) A food rich in iron
b) Three foods which give protein
c) Too much of this is bad for your teeth
d) This type has no fat in it
e) This type of bread has more fibre
f) Use this on your bread if you are trying to lose weight
g) This gives you strong bones and teeth

LIVER
CHEESE, FISH, MEAT
SUGAR
SKIMMED MILK
WHOLEMEAL
LOW FAT SPREAD

CALCIUM

5 **COMPLETE THE CROSSWORD TO DISCOVER DIFFERENT WAYS OF COOKING FOOD**

CLUES

ACROSS
2. Means to cook or steal fish. (5)
4. Sort out the mixed up girl and add an 'l'. (5)
5. Cook this way and you will increase the fat content. (3)
7. Cook using water vapour. (5)
8. Cook the Sunday lunch this way. (5)

DOWN
1. Water will do this at 100°c. (4)
3. Cook or reheat food in this way if you are in a hurry. (9)
6. A pie, biscuit or cake, put it in the oven to _____. (4)
7. Meat and vegetables cooked slowly in a pan. (4)

6 See how many words you can make from the words HEALTHY DIET.
You must use each letter once only in each new word.

7 In the wordsearch below you will find the name of the five main nutrient groups and two sources of each. Use the words to complete the table.
The words may be found in straight lines running horizontally, vertically, diagonally, forward or backward.

P	T	K	L	I	M	C	L	P	C	R	S
O	R	S	E	N	I	D	R	A	S	V	Q
T	E	O	N	P	R	S	R	M	V	S	C
A	F	A	T	O	T	R	E	Q	X	P	S
T	R	V	I	E	O	N	O	K	P	I	Q
O	S	I	L	T	I	R	T	I	A	H	U
E	V	T	S	W	X	N	A	D	Y	C	X
S	L	A	R	E	N	I	M	N	A	H	I
B	S	M	N	M	D	L	K	E	G	J	G
T	U	I	C	Q	R	V	E	Y	F	E	X
O	P	N	B	U	T	T	E	R	W	Y	S
Z	N	S	O	P	R	T	E	V	T	S	U
C	A	R	B	O	H	Y	D	R	A	T	E

NUTRIENT   **FOOD SOURCE**

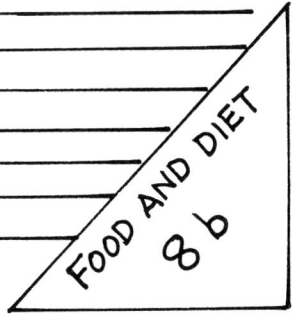

_____ < _____
_____ < _____
_____ < _____
_____ < _____
_____ < _____

FOOD AND DIET

8 b

Packing for a Picnic

There's nothing worse than soggy sandwiches, leaking lemonade, broken biscuits and pulverised plums. What a picnic! The packing was obviously a disaster.

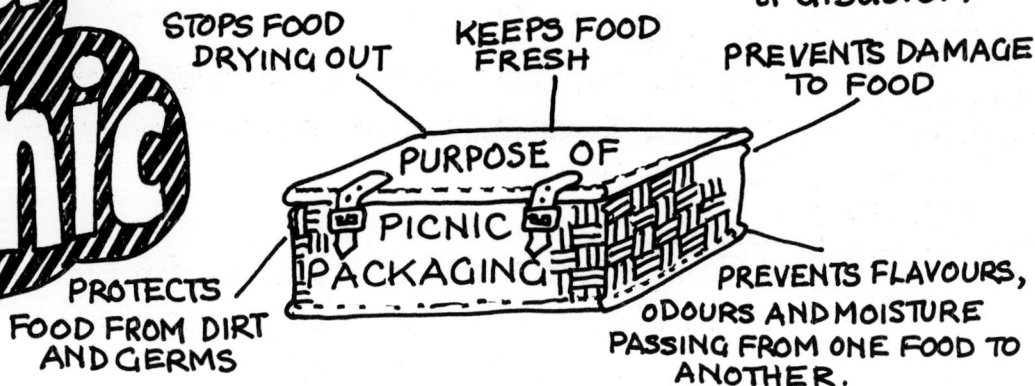

STOPS FOOD DRYING OUT

KEEPS FOOD FRESH

PREVENTS DAMAGE TO FOOD

PURPOSE OF PICNIC PACKAGING

PROTECTS FOOD FROM DIRT AND GERMS

PREVENTS FLAVOURS, ODOURS AND MOISTURE PASSING FROM ONE FOOD TO ANOTHER.

Use <u>some</u> of the given words to complete the rules to remember when choosing packaging for picnic foods.

CARRIED
GLASS
SPILLAGE
FRESH
HEAVY
DIRTY
SEAL
SQUARE
BREAKABLE

1. A picnic often has to be transported so _____ materials, e.g. _____ are not very suitable.

2. If the picnic has to be _____ bulky, _____ packaging materials are unsuitable.

3. All packaging must _____ well to lessen the risk of _____.

Unscramble the letters to reveal a list of packaging materials.

PPERA GBA _____   NICGL IMLF _____

SICTALP OXB _____   CUTIIBS INT _____

LGSAS TOTELB _____   ISPALTC OBTLTE _____

SFALK _____   MALIUMNUI OFIL _____

TAPICSL ABG _____   LIAPSCT BUT _____

Sort these materials into two groups – suitable packaging for a picnic and unsuitable packaging for a picnic.

Devise two picnics – one for a hillwalk on a cold December day and the other for an outing to the beach, travelling by car.

Swap your suggested picnics with a classmate. Choose suitable packaging materials for each of the foods in your classmate's picnics.

SOLVE THE SOGGY SANDWICHES

Certain sandwich fillings make the bread soggy if prepared in advance as picnic sandwiches are. Suggest some original and appetizing sandwich fillings for perfect picnic sandwiches.

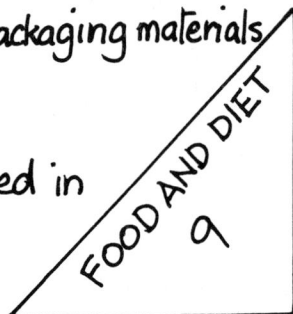

FOOD AND DIET

9

Teenage Diet Dominoes

As a teenager you have to choose your food carefully. Your body is changing and you need to eat the correct foods to cope with these changes.

Play Teenage Diet Dominoes to find out of which nutrients you need to eat more and in which foods you will find these nutrients.

RULES

1. Four players each pick up seven dominoes.
2. One player is chosen to play first and he/she lays down one of his/her dominoes.
3. The player to his/her left then lays down a domino which matches one end of the domino on the table. Dominoes may be matched as follows.
   1) nutrient and its job <u>to</u> food providing nutrient.
   2) food providing nutrient <u>to</u> nutrient of which teenager requires extra.
   3) nutrient of which teenager requires extra <u>to</u> nutrient and its job.
   4) If a player has no matching domino he misses a turn.
   5) The first player to lay down all his dominoes is declared the winner.

<u>Before the game</u> complete the dominoes marked with ★ using these words and diagrams.

PROTEIN   IRON
CARBOHYDRATE   CALCIUM
FAT   BONES
INFECTIONS

<u>After the game</u> answer these questions.

1. Why should a lazy teenager avoid eating too much carbohydrate?
2. Which nutrient is required to strengthen bones?
3. Suggest five food sources of protein.
4. Why might a teenage girl become anaemic?
5. Name two foods in which fat is hidden (ie it can't be seen).
6. Name two nutrients found in broccoli.
7. Give two reasons why a teenager might avoid fried foods.

CUT UP THE DOMINOES AND PLAY "TEENAGE DIET DOMINOES FOLLOWING THE GIVEN RULES.

FOOD AND DIET
10a

Dominoes (left column)

Treacle gives the body iron.

Teenagers often catch colds and other infections so they should eat plenty of vitamins.

★ keeps the blood healthy.

Chips give the body fat.

Fish gives the body protein.

Vitamins protect the body from infections and keep a teenager in good health.

Fried foods contain a lot of fat.

Fresh vegetables give the body vitamins.

★ give us carbohydrate.

Teenage girls lose blood during monthly periods so need extra iron.

helps ___ to build strong bones and teeth. ★

Cream and chocolate contain ___ fat.

Iron keeps the blood healthy

___ give the body vitamins ★

Teenagers who enjoy sports need plenty of carbohydrates for energy

Bread gives energy in the form of carbohydrate.

Protein helps the body to grow and repairs it when necessary.

Crisps contain a lot of ___ fat

Fat provides the body with heat.

Red meat gives the body iron.

Active teenagers use up lots of energy so need extra carbohydrate.

Milk provides calcium

Vitamins protect the body from ___ ★

If a teenager eats too much fat he may become overweight.

Carbohydrate provides ___ energy for the body.

Liver and kidney give the body iron

Fat gives the body heat but can cause greasy skin and hair if too much is eaten.

Eggs give us protein.

Calcium builds and strengthens bones and teeth.

Extra calcium is needed to help a teenagers bones to grow.

Teenagers who are not active may get too fat if they eat too many ___ foods. ★

A teenager may become anaemic if she does not get enough iron in her food.

Margarine gives the body fat

___ gives the body protein. ★

Fresh vegetables especially cabbage, broccoli and cauliflower contain iron.

Protein helps the body grow.

Yogurt is a rich source of calcium.

Plain chocolate gives the body iron.

Teenagers sometimes have greasy skin and spots so they should eat less ___ ★

Margarine gives the body vitamins

___ gives the body fat. ★

grow rapidly during the teenage years so extra calcium is needed.

Lentils and beans give the body ___ protein.

Black pudding gives the body iron.

A teenager who has an accident and loses blood will need extra iron. ★

A teenager grows rapidly and needs extra ___ to help his body to grow. ★

Carbohydrate provides energy for the body to work

A teenager who suffers from greasy skin and spots should eat less fat.

Vitamins help to protect teenagers from colds and infections which spread at school.

___ gives the body calcium.

Bread gives energy in the form of carbohydrate

Calcium strengthens a growing teenagers bones.

Rice, pasta and potatoes provide carbohydrate.

Teenage girls need extra iron to replace that lost during monthly periods.

Protein is essential during the growth spurt experienced by teenagers.

Too many carbohydrate foods may make an inactive teenager fat.

PROBLEMS FOR THE PLUMPS

Not only does being overweight take away some of the enjoyment of life, it can also shorten life by contributing to ill health and disease.

Match up each of the problems listed below with the appropriate member of the Plump family. Each member of the family may experience more than one problem.

THE PLUMP FAMILY

GRANNY PLUMP

MR. PLUMP

MRS. PLUMP

PATRICK PLUMP
(14 YEARS OLD)

PENELOPE PLUMP
(5 YEARS OLD)

PROBLEMS OF BEING OVERWEIGHT

- I cannot run about quickly when we play football so I'm not in the school team.

- Other little boys and girls laugh at me and call me names.

- I always wanted to get a job as a slater but could not climb about easily so had to take a boring office job.

- The doctor says that I am more at risk of getting arthritis and varicose veins than other old people.

- I cannot fit on the slides and swings in the playpark.

- I get very depressed when I see slim people trying on nice dresses as I know that I cannot wear them.

- A man of my age, especially an overweight man, is at risk of having a heart attack.

- Girls will not dance with me at the disco.

- I seldom go into china and gift shops as I tend to knock things over.

- I tend to sit in the house a lot as walking is very tiring for me.

Choose one of Granny Plump's problems and illustrate it with a diagram. Repeat this for the other members of the Plump family.

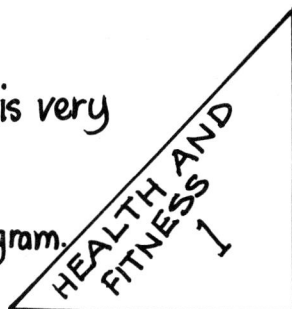

HEALTH AND FITNESS 1

The Plump family want to become a fit family. To do so they will have to lose weight. Weight loss is speeded up by exercising.

FITNESS IS FUN

HELP THE PLUMP FAMILY TO GET INTO SHAPE BY SOLVING THEIR PROBLEMS.

☆ Mr. Plump works five days a week from 9am. to 12.30pm and from 1.30pm to 5.30pm.

He is keen to take up some sports.
What could he play and when could he play?

☆ A day in the life of Mrs. Plump

8.00 – 8.30am.	Eat breakfast
8.30 – 10.00a.m.	housework
10.00 – 11.00a.m.	coffee and cakes with friends.
11.00 – 1.00pm.	catch bus to and from shops
1.00 – 1.45pm.	lunch
1.45 – 2.30p.m.	watch television; afternoon tea and cakes
2.30 – 3.00p.m.	catch bus to local school to meet Penelope.

Mrs. Plump's day includes very little exercise. What changes could she make to increase the amount of exercise?
Write her a "Get Fit" timeplan for a day.

☆ Granny Plump spends most of her time sitting watching television. What gentle forms of exercise could she take up?

☆ Patrick and Penelope Plump have always avoided all sports and games at school and at home.

They will both have to start taking part in P.E at school. Suggest some other forms of exercise for each of them.

☆ Exercising together can be fun.
What forms of exercise could the Plumps take up as a family?
(Maybe Granny will have to miss out on some!)

HEALTH AND FITNESS 2

BODY TALK

Using magazines cut out adverts for body care products which you might use. Try to find at least one for each part of your body, e.g. hair, face, nails.

Explain how and why you would use each product.

What is your favourite pop song?

Sing it to yourself (silently!!) and make up an exercise routine which fits your song. Your exercises should make each moveable part of your body work, e.g. neck, feet, fingers.

Describe or illustrate your exercise routine.

Example

Raise both arms
10 times

Jog on spot to count
of 100

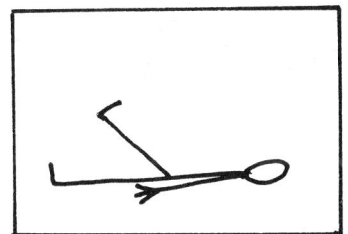

Lift each leg
10 times

Find out and describe how you would deal with three of the following body problems:

athlete's foot	head lice
sunburn	ingrown toe nail

HEALTHY HOLIDAY?

We hear about health farms but few of us actually go to them.

Write an account of what you imagine a weekend at a health farm would be like. Don't forget to describe the activities and the food.

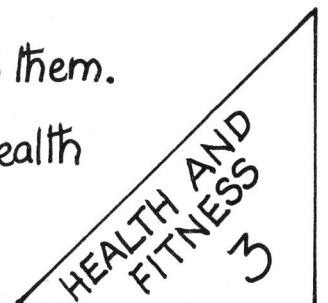

HEALTH AND FITNESS 3

BE A SPORT

It is the last lap and Gordon Kwikfeet of Great Britain is in third place. 100 m. to go and he has moved into second place. "Will he make it? 20 m. to go and it is neck and neck. Could this be the first gold medal for Great Britain? Yes, Gordon Kwikfeet has won the gold medal.

Choose your favourite sportsperson and pretend that you are his/her coach leading up to a major event.

Make an information booklet for the person.

Remember to make your booklet colourful, attractive and interesting.

Give your sportsperson advice on the following topics.

(a) EXERCISE ROUTINE: Write a programme for your sportsperson which could include warm up exercises, fitness training for his/her particular sport and most importantly the need for rest and relaxation.

(b) BODY MATTERS You want to be proud of your sportsperson so appearance is important. Include information on bathing/showering, hygiene products, changing of clothes and problems particular to his/her sport, e.g. athletes foot.

(c) CLOTHES CONSCIOUS

① Recommend suitable fabrics for sports clothes giving reasons for your choice.

② Choose outfits from magazines or catalogues and stick them in your booklet or be adventurous and design your own.

(d) SPORTING FOODS

① List the important nutrients required by your sportsperson and suggest suitable foods.

② Plan a menu for a day for your chosen sportsperson.

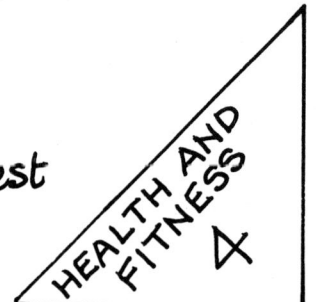

HEALTH AND FITNESS

With the right equipment and a little enthusiasm cleaning can be done quickly and easily.

It is easier to do a job if you know how to do it properly.

• Match each cleaning item with the correct statement.

Do not mix these as it can be very dangerous.

Wear these to protect hands from strong cleaning fluids.

Cleans, protects and gives a shiny finish to wooden furniture.

Use on baths and sinks.

Kills germs in sinks, baths and toilets.

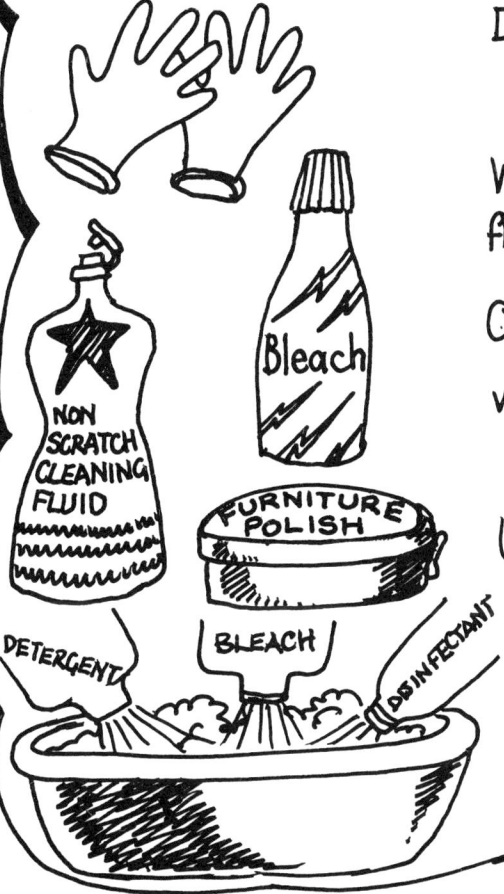

On a self-catering holiday you are expected to look after the accommodation as if it were your own home, leaving it clean and tidy ready for the next people.

• Look at the picture of the self-catering holiday home.

☆ Show which jobs are necessary in each room by drawing the appropriate symbols in that room.

☆ Decide which cleaning materials are going to be required to do these jobs and draw these into the appropriate rooms.

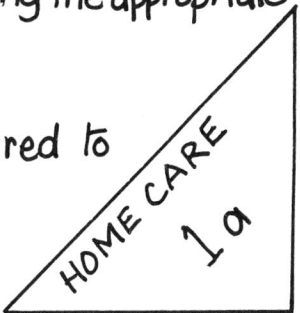

HOME CARE 1a

JOBS

HOOVER

WIPE

DUST

SWEEP

MOP

TIDY UP

 EMPTY BINS

CLEANING MATERIALS

SPRAY POLISH

BLEACH

NON-SCRATCH LIQUID/CREAM

DISINFECTANT

HOME CARE 1b

SWEET DREAMS

Setting up and furnishing a house involves a lot of planning and is very expensive. Try doing just one room - your dream bedroom.

Draw a plan of the bedroom as you would like it. Include all furniture and soft furnishings - curtains, bed linen, lampshades, cushions, and don't forget a carpet. Use coloured pencils to show your chosen colour scheme.

To find the approximate cost of furnishing your dream bedroom

1. collect a mail order catalogue

2. look up the prices of the furniture and soft furnishings you have chosen.
(You will probably not find exactly what you want in the catalogue so take the prices of the items most similar to your chosen ones)

3. add up the total cost of furnishing your dream bedroom.

Now imagine the cost of furnishing your dream house!

HOME CARE 2

Rubbish Recycled

Is your dustbin really full of rubbish? Think before you answer! Is it actually rubbish or could some of it be used again in an attempt to make the world's natural resources last longer?

CONSERVATION CHALLENGE

Design one or more household articles using items which would normally be discarded. You may like to choose a household article from the list below but feel free to use your own ideas.

lampshade   room tidy

table mat   desk tidy

toaster cover

wall decoration

plant pot holder

cushion cover

CLASS CHALLENGE

Choose the best ideas for household articles and produce some of each. Sell them and put the proceeds to good use, for example, planting new trees.

HOME CARE 3

Designer Dilemma

Certain household items have to be functional as well as appealing to the eye. This can cause problems for the designers. Bearing this in mind, see if you can design

- a toothbrush holder which keeps the heads of the toothbrushes clean

- a dish/plate from which you would eat soup and bread

- attractive storage jars of one size which stack and therefore take up little space when empty

CONSUMER 1

COMMERCIAL CAPERS

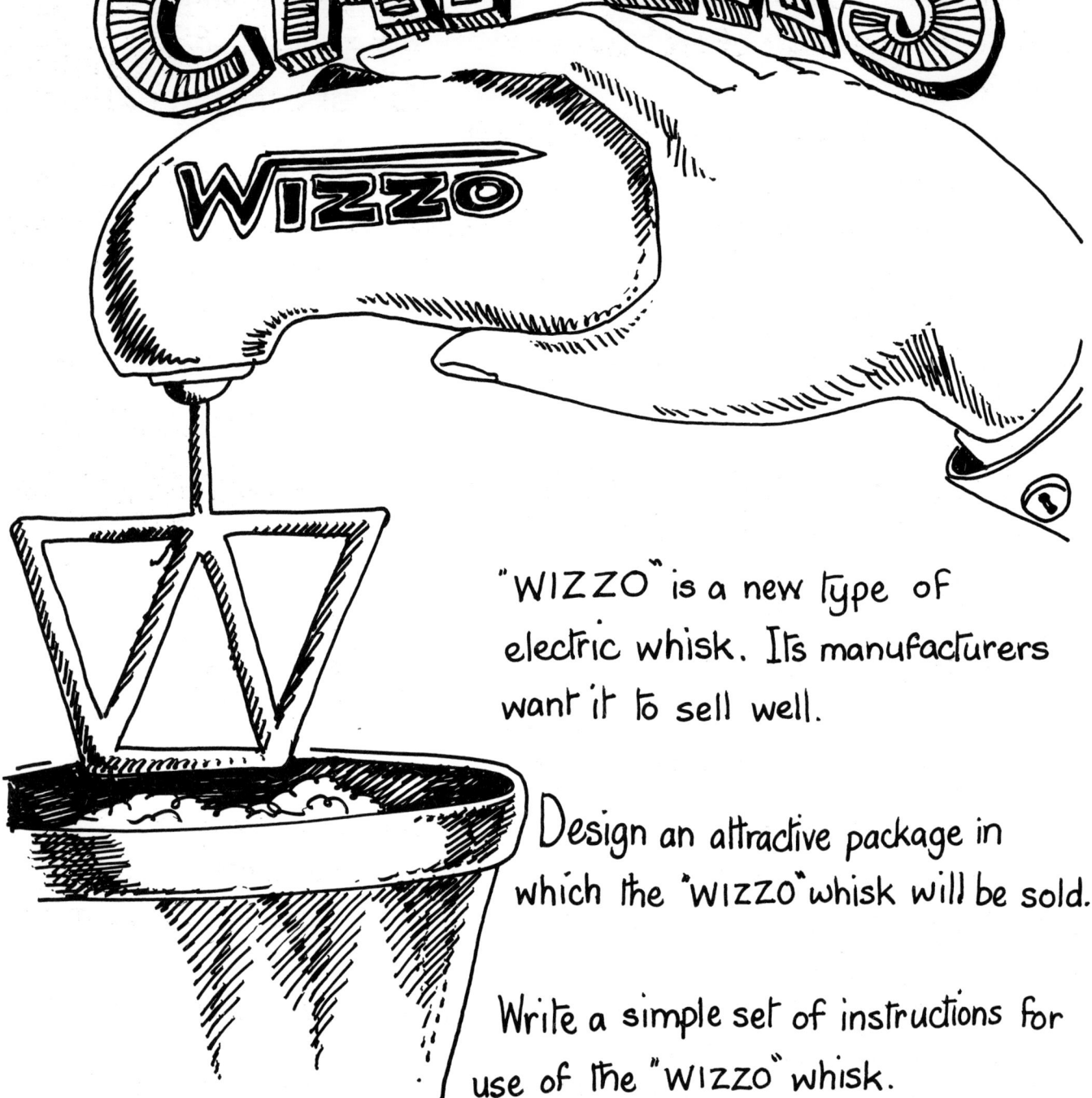

WIZZO

"WIZZO" is a new type of electric whisk. Its manufacturers want it to sell well.

Design an attractive package in which the "WIZZO" whisk will be sold.

Write a simple set of instructions for use of the "WIZZO" whisk.

Get together with a few classmates and make up a television commercial to advertise the whisk. Act out the commercial for the rest of the class.

CONSUMER 2

COSTA DEL PACKET

Sun, sea, sand, lazy days – – – – – – – – dreaming of a holiday.

A holiday is a luxury, however and money cannot be put aside to pay for it until all the "essentials of life" have been paid for.

Seven of the "essentials of life" are hidden in the wordsearch. See if you can find them. The words may be found in straight lines running horizontally, vertically, diagonally, forward or backwards.

J	T	A	R	U	A	L	F	O	F	S	N	G	E
Y	T	R	M	U	A	I	X	O	T	R	J	E	G
R	L	C	A	E	L	E	O	E	H	P	I	C	N
G	A	S	R	N	T	D	V	Q	M	B	D	G	I
A	T	V	M	E	S	E	H	T	O	L	C	Z	S
N	H	Q	N	K	N	P	A	D	A	O	J	B	U
I	D	C	E	A	B	I	O	E	B	W	F	N	O
V	I	P	P	E	C	N	A	R	U	S	N	I	H
E	L	E	C	T	R	I	C	I	T	Y	O	U	O

Holiday Spending

☆ Before planning or booking a holiday you must know how much money you can afford to spend.

☆ Use the picture clues to work out what your holiday money will be spent on.

USE TRAVEL BROCHURES TO CHOOSE:

☆ a two week self-catering holiday in the sun for four people in August.

☆ a skiing holiday for two people who want to stay in a hotel for a week in February.

☆ a holiday in the sun for a couple and their baby who wish to share a hotel room for two weeks in October.

For each holiday give the following information: name of resort, facilities offered in local area, cost of holiday.

VALUE FOR MONEY ☆ ☆ ☆ ☆ ☆ ☆ ☆

Having spent your hard-earned money on a holiday you will want to get good value for that money. You are entitled to exactly what you have paid for in transport, accommodation and facilities. Do not accept less! Explain exactly what you would do if your holiday did not turn out to be what you had booked and paid for.

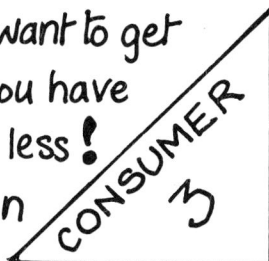

CONSUMER 3

TEENAGE TEMPTATIONS

You have decided to organise your own mail order catalogue for teenagers. To help you make decisions about your catalogue look through several existing catalogues and write comments on their good and bad points as far as teenagers are concerned.

A NEW STYLE CATALOGUE
- Give your catalogue a name.
- Make a list of the items to be sold.
- Draw an advert for your catalogue and suggest places where it could be seen.
- Now make up an advert to be heard on radio.

You will need to draw up very strict guidelines for catalogue owners.

From the list below tick those which will apply

Incentives to sell would be :
▶ reduced prices for catalogue owners
▶ free records for introducing friends as catalogue owners
▶ monthly disco for owners meeting sales targets

New catalogue published :
▶ every week
▶ every month
▶ two / three / four times a year

Spending limits :
▶ set by parents or guardians
▶ set at 50 pence
▶ set by catalogue owners

Failure to pay will be dealt with by :
▶ asking parents to pay teenagers' debts
▶ reclaiming items ordered
▶ taking non-payer to court

ADD ANY OTHER GUIDELINES YOU THINK ARE NECESSARY

SANTA CRUZ   PHOTOS

CONSUMER 4

NOEL, NOEL

Christmas is fast approaching and Mr. Noel will have to buy a Christmas present for each member of his family.

Mr. Noel has been saving money each month since last Christmas and has managed to save £150. The money is in a building society so it has been earning interest.

✴ Why are your savings better in a bank or building society account than in a piggy bank?

✴ Find out why banks and building societies can afford to pay interest to their savers?

✴ Mr. Noel's money has earned 10% interest over the year. Work out how much money Mr. Noel has to spend on Christmas presents.

✴ Using catalogues choose Mr. Noel's presents for his family.

✴ Draw and describe each present, state for whom it is chosen and its price. (Remember Mr. Noel's spending limit.)

✴ State how much Mr. Noel has spent.

Mr. Nojoy, Mr. Noel's neighbour, has not saved any money for Christmas but he still has to buy presents. What a predicament! How is he going to buy presents if he has no money saved?

As it happens Mr. Nojoy is in luck. He has a <u>credit card</u> therefore he will be able to buy the presents, have them right away but pay for them later.

✴ Why is a credit card a useful thing to have?

✴ From whom would Mr. Nojoy obtain his credit card?

Unfortunately if Mr. Nojoy does not pay his credit card bill within a certain time limit he will be charged interest on the money he has borrowed. The company from which Mr. Nojoy has his credit card charges an interest rate of 25%. Imagine that Mr. Nojoy has to buy exactly the same presents as Mr. Noel. Obviously he will have to use his credit card and will not be able to pay back the money within the time limit given. ✴ Work out how much Mr. Nojoy will have to pay for the presents.

✴ What are the disadvantages of having a credit card?

✴ Find out as much as you can about other ways in which Mr. Nojoy could have borrowed money to buy his presents.

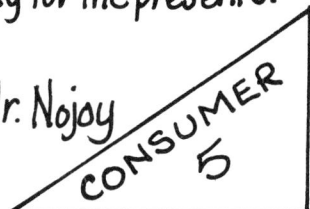

CONSUMER 5

ALL THE FUN OF THE FAIR

The local hospital urgently requires funds to buy life-saving equipment.

Your class has decided to run a fair to raise money. If it is to be a success the fair will have to be very well organised.

The class should devise several plans for the fair then choose the best ideas.

Working in a group, follow these guidelines to produce your plan.

GUIDELINES

1. Choose a theme for the fair, e.g. Victorian Fair, Walt Disney Fair, etc. This will give your fair individuality and attract customers.

2. Make a list of jobs to be done before the fair and a list of those to be done on the day of the fair.

   (If possible seek advice from somebody who has organised a successful fair in the past.)

3. Bearing in mind your theme, plan the stalls listing items to be sold on each stall. Try to give each stall an imaginative name instead of the usual "Cake and Candy", "Bric-a-brac".

You should now have a basic plan for the fair so it is time for action.

(Make use of individual talents within the group, e.g. artistic and mathematical talents.) Start with some of the following jobs:

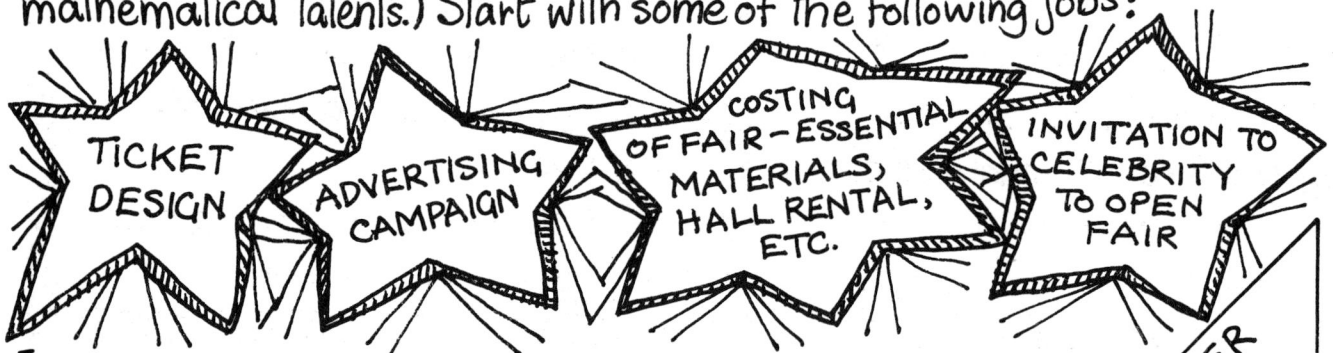

TICKET DESIGN

ADVERTISING CAMPAIGN

COSTING OF FAIR – ESSENTIAL MATERIALS, HALL RENTAL, ETC.

INVITATION TO CELEBRITY TO OPEN FAIR

If possible choose the best plan for a fair and, as a class, run that fair. Donate the proceeds to a worthy cause.

CONSUMER 6a

ALL THE FUN OF THE FAIR

Home baking is always a good money maker. Read the recipes below and give each a name which relates to the theme of your fair.

300g plain chocolate
45 ml golden syrup
25g butter
225g swiss style breakfast
    cereal muesli

Melt 150g chocolate with the golden syrup and butter.
Stir in the muesli and mix thoroughly.
Press into a shallow 20cm square tin.
Melt remaining chocolate and spread over the muesli mixture.
Mark with a fork and chill until set.
Cut into fingers or square pieces.
NB Milk chocolate may be used if preferred.   Makes 20

600g soft bananas
2×5ml bicarbonate of soda
200g margarine
300g sugar
1×5ml spoon vanilla essence
2 eggs
600g plain flour
2×5ml spoons baking powder
200g chopped walnuts
280g milk approx.

Mix bananas and bicarbonate of soda and leave aside.
Beat margarine and sugar until white
Mix banana mixture into margarine and sugar. Gradually add the beaten eggs.
Add some flour if the mixture appears curdled. Add remaining flour.
Fold in nuts and milk until mixture is of a soft consistency and place into 3 prepared tins.
Bake at 190°c/Gas 5 for 1¼ hrs approx.
Makes 3 × 450gm loaves.

250g SR Flour
200g margarine
200g soft brown sugar
200g salted peanuts (crushed)

Mix margarine and sugar until light and fluffy. Add flour and nuts. Divide mixture into equal size pieces. Form into small balls and press down with a fork. Place on greased baking sheets. Cook in preheated oven 180°c/Gas 4 for 20 minutes.
Makes 36

Work out the cost of the ingredients of each recipe. You have decided that you want to make 50% profit. Work out the price of each item sold.   CONSUMER 6b

ON THE TOUCH LINE

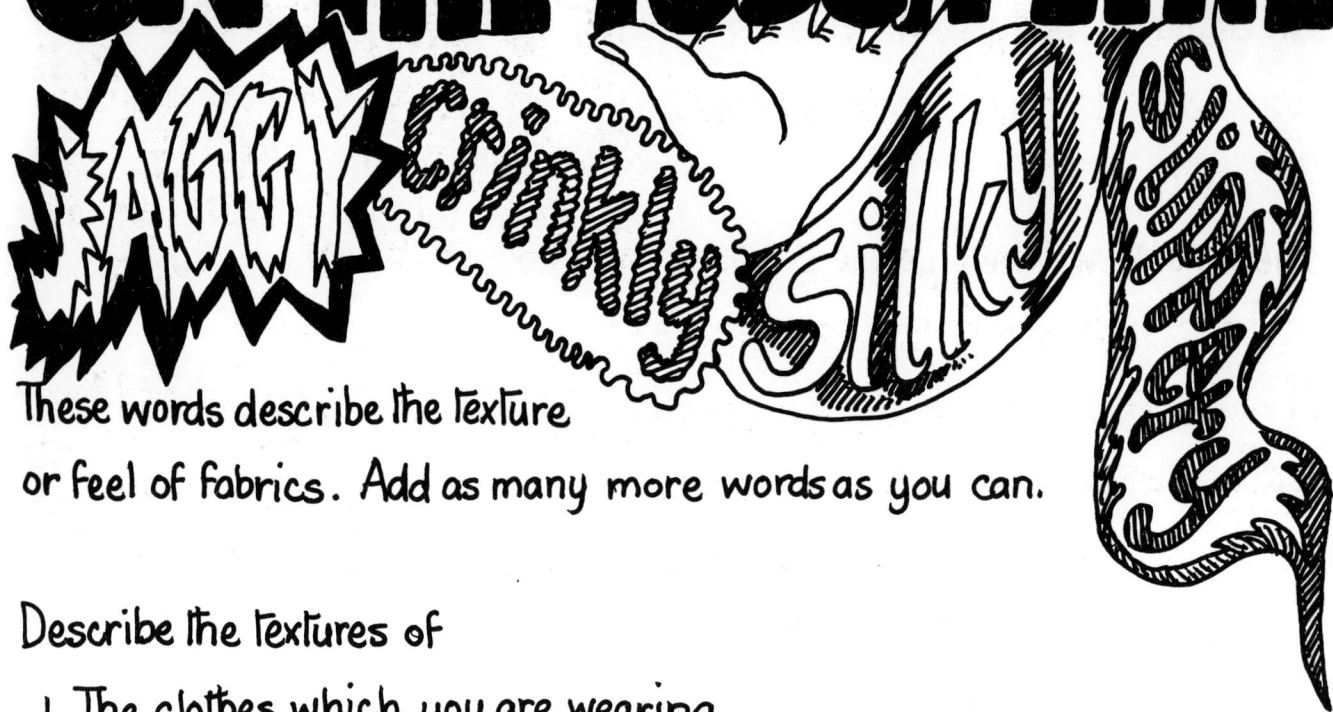

JAGGY **crinkly** **Silky** *slippery*

These words describe the texture or feel of fabrics. Add as many more words as you can.

Describe the textures of

1. The clothes which you are wearing.

2. Any other fabrics in the room.

Draw arrows to match the textures and items given below

TEXTURES:
Slippery, fine (thin)
ribbed
rough
soft
smooth

ITEMS
baby's sleepsuit
kagoul
cord trousers
carpet tile
silk tie

COMPLETE THE FOLLOWING TABLE

	SAMPLE OF FABRIC WITH A SUITABLE TEXTURE	REASONS FOR CHOICE OF FABRIC
A SPORTS BAG		
A NIGHTSHIRT		
A BEANBAG		
A SPORTS TOP		

FABRIC AND CLOTHES CARE 1

By choosing clothes carefully you can disguise body faults, for example, wide hips, very small chest, lack of height.

These rules will help you to choose clothes which will flatter your faults!

|||| Vertical stripes make your body appear slimmer and taller. ||||

☰ Horizontal stripes make your body appear plumper and shorter. ☰

▶◀ Dark colours have a slimming effect. ▶◀

◥◣ Light colours make your body appear larger. ◥◣

FAULT FLATTERY

Disguise these body faults by drawing suitable clothes onto the figures.
Remember you can use different rules for different parts of the body.

Wide-hipped Wendy dressing for a wedding.

Tall thin Timothy going to a disco

Chubby-chested Calum wearing a tracksuit for football training

Short stubby Samantha going to a pop concert.

Describe your own body shape, pointing out any faults which you want to disguise. Draw or cut from catalogues some clothes which would flatter your faults.

FABRIC AND CLOTHES CARE 2

A STITCH IN TIME

Follow these instructions to make a useful Summer Smile Mend-It Kit to take on your holidays or carry around daily.

Requirements

1 double circle of felt	2 pins
1 safety pin	80 cm black thread
2 small buttons	80 cm White thread
1 needle	thread to sew on buttons

INSTRUCTIONS

1. Sew the buttons onto the outside of one half of the felt circles as if they are eyes. (Check with your teacher or a book to be sure that you know how to sew on buttons correctly.)

2. Attach the safety pin to the same piece of felt, placing it in position as a mouth.

3. Open up the Mend-It Kit and into the inside of the lower circle stick the pins and the needle.

4. Wind the black thread around one of the pins in a figure of eight. (Be careful not to pull it too tightly.) Wind the white thread around the other pin in the same way.

FABRIC AND CLOTHES CARE
3

COMPETITION
Design for a Star

Win a weekend at the recording studio of a pop group/star of your choice.

HOW TO ENTER : Design outfits for your favourite pop star or members of your favourite pop group for their next British Tour.

CLOSING DATE FOR ENTRY 6th APRIL

DRESS TO IMPRESS

Together with friends you have already made a list of points to be considered when entering this competition.

- fans want to copy their idols' outfits
- pop stars get very warm during television recordings and concerts
- outfits will have to be washed or dry cleaned.
- outfits must not restrict movement

Today is the 29th of March. You have only a few days left to enter the competition. Write down any more points to be considered when designing your outfits.

★ State which group/star the outfits are for. ★ Draw the outfits ready for posting. ★

As well as designing the outfits you have decided to show how their hair will be styled, the colour and style of makeup if worn, and any accessories they will wear.

You will surely be a winner.

CONGRATULATIONS! You have won first prize in the "Design for a Star" competition.

Your teacher has asked you to give a short talk to the class about your winning entry.

FABRIC AND CLOTHES CARE

Deciding which of your clothes to take on holiday is difficult. Maybe you would be better putting your wardrobe on wheels and taking it along! However, you must make the choice. Tick or write down the factors which you would consider when choosing :

• method of transport, e.g. train, walking

• whether the clothes crush easily

• the cost of the holiday   • amount of luggage allowed.

• what you will be doing on holiday • the weather

• what your friends are taking on their holidays

• whether the hotel/campsite is large or small

   Explain why you would consider each of these factors.

For each holiday listed choose a suitable set of clothes and bag from those shown below, (you may use a bag more than once.)
Explain your choices.

Walking holiday in Northern Scotland   Cycling holiday in France
Watersports holiday in Portugal   Tour of Wales in a caravan
Skiing holiday in Switzerland   Beach holiday in Spain

If you had a free choice, what type of holiday would you go on? Draw or cut from a catalogue a suitable set of clothes for your chosen holiday.

FABRIC AND CLOTHES CARE
5a

HOTEL
5th floor

WALKING WARDROBE 2

Imagine that you are going to make your own holiday clothes. Depending on the type of holiday you are going on you will possibly need clothes which:

• are waterproof

• do not crush easily

• are able to absorb moisture easily (so that if you sweat in hot weather or while playing a sport the sweat will be absorbed by the clothes instead of lying on your skin).

Carry out the tests below on a range of fabrics then choose a suitable fabric for each of the following

★ a waterproof jacket

★ a shirt which will not crush

★ a sports top.

Crush Test
1. Crush fabric sample in your hand.
2. Count to 100.
3. Release fabric and examine for creases.

Waterproof Test
1. Onto your fabric sample drop a few drops of water.
2. Watch closely to see whether the water sinks in, runs through or sits on the surface of the fabric.
3. If the water sits on the surface the fabric is waterproof.

Moisture Absorption Test
1. Onto your fabric sample drop a few drops of water.
2. Watch closely to see whether the water sits on the surface, runs through the fabric or sinks in and remains in the fabric.
3. If the water sinks in and remains in the fabric the sample absorbs moisture easily.

Cut a small sample of each of your chosen fabrics. Stick the samples beside drawings of your own designs for the jacket, shirt and sports top.

FABRIC AND CLOTHES CARE
56

COMMUNITY SPIRIT

A community is a group of people who live in the same area. Obviously a community includes people of all ages and types.

Make a study of one of these community groups

ELDERLY   HANDICAPPED/DISABLED

TEENAGERS PRE-SCHOOL CHILDREN

Produce an information booklet about your chosen group.

GUIDELINES:

1. Read books and leaflets to find out about your chosen group.

2. Use diagrams and colour to make your study interesting and appealing.

3. Give your study an original title.

4. Use the following as section headings for your booklet if you wish.

SPECIAL NEEDS PROBLEMS

SERVICES PROVIDED WHAT OTHERS CAN DO TO HELP.

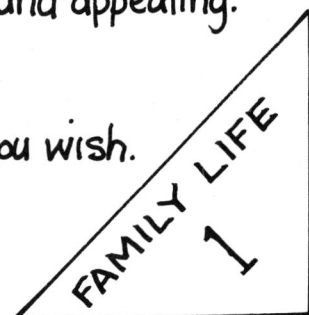

FAMILY LIFE 1

ONE OF THE GANG

Write a story with the title "One of the Gang" based on an idea suggested by one of the pictures below.

PICK'N'M

CLOSED

EVENTIDE HOME FOR THE ELDERLY

WINE

LAGER

VIDEOS FOR HIRE AND SALE

SOAP

OZONE FRIENDLY DEODORANT

FAMILY LIFE 2

BLACK MAGIC

Everyone enjoys a party - everyone that is apart from the host or hostess, who is usually worrying about whether or not the party is a success.

The way to ensure that a party is successful is to plan it well.

PLAN A HALLOWEEN PARTY FOR A GROUP OF 8 TO 10 YEAR OLDS.

Your party plan must include the following:

① A programme of events. Complete the one below.

6.30 p.m.	Witches and Wizards Name Game
6.40 p.m.	The Haunted House
6.55 p.m.	
.	
.	
.	
8.00 p.m.	Supper around the cauldron
.	
.	
9.00 p.m	Witches and Wizards fly home!

② The menu for supper around the cauldron.

③ A party invitation

④ A plan showing how the room will be decorated.

⑤ A mask to be worn at the party.

⑥ A decoration for the party room.

FAMILY LIFE 3

TOYING WITH TROUBLE

READ THE PASSAGE BELOW.

Emily raked in her toybox trying to choose some toys for her young brother Richard to play with. She cast aside her old teddy bear. Teddy's eyes had come loose a long time ago and could easily be pulled off and swallowed by Richard. The lego would appeal to Richard but again the small pieces may be swallowed. Small toys, buttons and eyes are often mistaken for sweets by young children. "Ah, the xylophone," thought Emily, "that's just what he would like. Oh, and that blue furry rabbit." She pulled them out from the bottom of the toybox and headed off downstairs to surprise Richard.

Emily did not get very far before bumping into her Dad who sent her right back to the toybox! Dad explained that the xylophone had very sharp edges and was painted with paint that was not lead free. Chewing that type of paint would do Richard no good and he may cut himself on the sharp edges. As for the rabbit- the ribbon around its neck looks very attractive but Richard might chew it and choke on it.

Emily trudged slowly back to the toybox and continued her search. Surely there must be at least one suitable toy for Richard in here!

① Draw the toys that are unsuitable for Richard. Explain why each is unsuitable.

② Draw or describe any other toys you think are too dangerous for young children to play with.

③ Young children need something to play with. Design a safe toy for a child's cot. Remember that children like toys that are brightly coloured, have moving parts and make different sounds.

FAMILY LIFE
4

TELL-TALE

You have been asked to read a story at the local playgroup and decide to make up your own book.

1. Decide on the type and size of your story book.

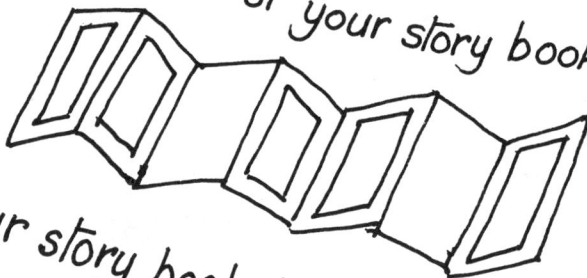

2. Decide of what your story book is going to be made, paper, card, etc.

3. Decide on a theme, that is, what the story will be about.

4. Write the story on the pages of your book. Remember to make the writing clear.

5. Use pictures from magazines or your own drawings to decorate your book.

Your book should be neat, colourful and interesting to keep the children's attention.

FAMILY LIFE
5

I LOVE TO GO A'WANDERING

You are going hillwalking with the local youth club.

You have to be at the youth club by 10 a.m.

The following is a list of things that must be done before leaving.

Prepare breakfast

Dry hair

Get up and shower

Clean walking boots

Prepare packed lunch

Eat breakfast

Pack backpack

Leave a copy of hillwalk route and emergency contact number.

Look up bus timetable for bus to youth club

Make up group first aid kit

Dress

① Estimate how long each task will take

eg. Get up and shower 10 mins

Dry hair 8 mins

You will then be able to decide what time you will need to get up in the morning.

② Now organise the tasks in a logical order and make a Time plan

e.g. 6·30 – 6·40 Get up and shower

6·40 – 6·48 Dry hair

③ Underline the tasks you could possibly do the night before. How much time would that save on the morning of the walk?

④ BACK PACK Make a list of the items you would have to take with you in your backpack.

FIRST AID You have been asked to make up the first aid kit for the group. Draw and name the items you would take.

LUNCH Decide what you should take for lunch and state how you would pack it, giving reasons for your choice.

FAMILY LIFE

6

It's Party Time

"Ring a Ring of Roses _____ The Farmer's in his den _____ The grand old Duke of York, crisps, presents, icecream, birthday cake," and I thought planning Lucy's 5th birthday party would be easy.

I asked Mum for some help but all she gave me was this mixed up list of jobs.

- set table
- order icecream
- make birthday cake
- make gift for each child to take home.

- prepare food
- post invitations
- collect ice cream
- make up programme of events.

- organise helpers.
- shop for food
- decorate birthday cake

I am not sure when each job should be done. Can you help me by placing each job under the correct heading?

WEEK BEFORE PARTY   DAY BEFORE PARTY   PARTY DAY

Now that I have got you involved perhaps you could help me by

(1) designing a biscuit Merry Go Round for the centre of the table.

   Draw the design and list the materials and ingredients required.

(2) making up a game which the children could play after they have eaten.

(3) making a thank-you card to send to each of the helpers.

FAMILY LIFE 7

ANSWER PAGE (1)

Safety.

③ The Search For Safety

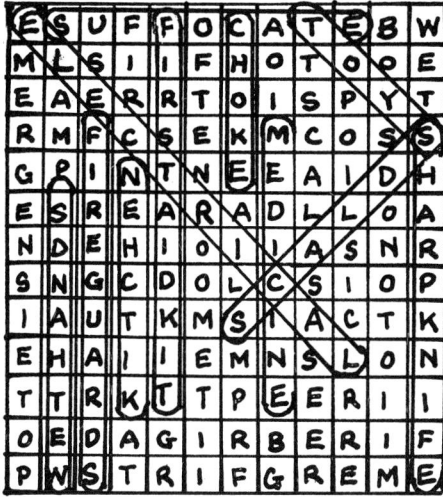

④ Be On Your Guard

Across   1. Insurance
           5. Heaters
           6. Water
           9. Doors and windows
           10. Burglars
           12. Valuables

Down   2. Electricity
           3. Neighbours
           4. Ladders
           7. Gas
           8. Police
           11. Plugs
           13. Alarm

Food and Diet

⑧ Let's Get Quizzical

1. Eggs, fish, lentils, milk, beans, nuts, cheese, meat
2. ⓐ pressure cooker ⓑ electric whisk ⓒ sharp knife ⓓ egg separator
   ⓔ grater ⓕ lemon squeezer
3. ⓐ strawberry ⓑ tomato ⓒ apricot ⓓ cauliflower ⓔ potato ⓕ cabbage
4. ⓐ liver ⓑ cheese, fish, meat ⓒ sugar ⓓ skimmed milk ⓔ wholemeal
   ⓕ low fat spread ⓖ calcium

5. Across   2. Poach
            4. Grill
            5. Fry
            7. Steam
            8. Roast
   Down   1. Boil
            3. Microwave
            6. Bake
            7. Stew

7.

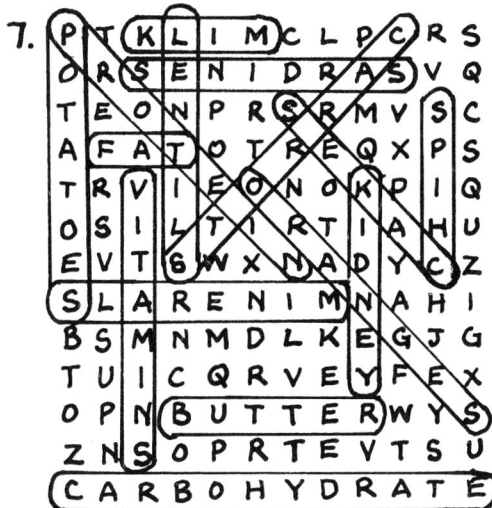

Nutrient	Food Source
Protein	• MILK
	• LENTILS
Fat	• CHIPS
	• BUTTER
Carbohydrate	• POTATOES
	• CAKES
Vitamins	• ORANGES
	• CARROTS
Minerals	• KIDNEY
	• SARDINES

ANSWER (2)

Home Care

(1) Spick 'n' Span

Wear these to protect hands from strong cleaning fluids ►

Kills germs in sinks, baths and toilets ►

Use on baths and sinks ►

Do not mix these as it can be very dangerous.

Cleans, protects and gives a shiny finish to wooden furniture ▼

Consumer

(3) Costa del Packet

The seven "essentials of life" are Food, Clothes, Housing, Transport, Gas, Electricity and Insurance.

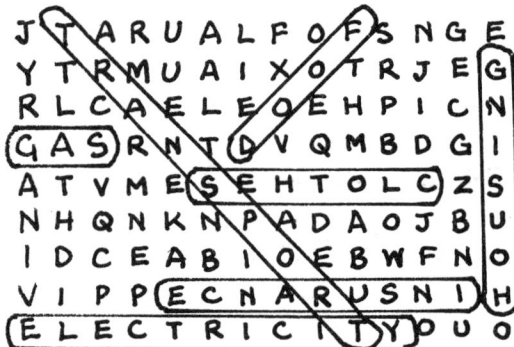

```
J T A R U A L F O F S N G E
Y T R M U A I X O T R J E G
R L C A E L E O E H P I C N
G A S R N T D V Q M B D G I
A T V M E S E H T O L C Z S
N H Q N K N P A D A O J B U
I D C E A B I O E B W F N O
V I P P E C N A R U S N I H
E L E C T R I C I T Y O U O
```

Fabric and Clothes Care   ① On the Touch Line

Baby's sleepsuit	►	soft
Kagoul	►	slippery, fine (thin) or smooth
Cord trousers	►	ribbed
Carpet tile	►	rough
Silk tie	►	smooth or slippery, fine (thin)